A Day With NEANDERTHAL MAN

LIFE 70,000 YEARS AGO

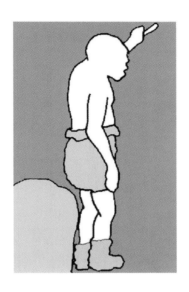

DR. FIORENZO FACCHINI

A Day With NEANDERTHAL MAN

LIFE 70,000 YEARS AGO

Illustrations by
ALESSANDRO BALDANZI

TWENTY-FIRST CENTURY BOOKS / BROOKFIELD, CONNECTICUT

English translation copyright © 2003 by Twenty-First Century Books
Originally published by Editoriale Jaca Book spa
Via Gioberti 7,
20123, Milano, Italy
www.jacabook.it

Library of Congress Cataloging-in-Publication Data
Facchini, Fiorenzo, 1929–
[Fiorenzo Facchini racconta la giornata di un uomo di Neandertal.
English]
A day with Neanderthal man : life 70,000 years ago / Fiorenzo Facchini;
illustrations by Alessandro Baldanzi.
p. cm. — (Early humans)
Translation of: Fiorenzo Facchini racconta la giornata di un uomo di Neandertal.
Includes index.
Summary: Describes an imaginary day in the life of a group of prehistoric people as they
obtain food, make tools, explore the world around them, and hold a funeral for a boy who
was not careful enough about what he ate.
ISBN 0-7613-2767-3 (lib. bdg.)
1. Neanderthals—Juvenile literature. [1. Neanderthals. 2. Prehistoric peoples.]
I. Baldanzi, Alessandro, ill. II. Title. III. Series.

GN285 .F3313 2003
569.9—dc21   2002152451

Published by Twenty-First Century Books
A Division of The Millbrook Press, Inc.
2 Old New Milford Road
Brookfield, Connecticut 06804
www.millbrookpress.com

Printed in Italy
2 4 5 3 1

CONTENTS

Foreword

6

Introduction

Entering the World of Neanderthal Man

7

Kawak's Day

19

Glossary

44

Index

47

Picture Credits

48

FOREWORD

In the volumes in this series that deal with the daily life of *Homo habilis* and *Homo erectus,* arrows point toward pictures which are far, in time and space, from the protagonist's story. In this story, in which Homo sapiens neanderthalensis is the main character, we will also see arrows. They will call our attention to elements of human life that will become more important as humankind develops.

It is possible that burials were first used during the time of Neanderthal. The graves made by Neanderthal humans reveal a new way of thinking about death and about beginnings and endings in general. Certainly, the life cycles of animals and the change of seasons gave humans reasons to reflect upon this concept.

Going forward, arrows will point out objects, animals, and customs that show up, in the future of mankind, in various artistic forms as evidence of culture. These bear witness to the human need to gather and interpret signs from nature and from the surrounding environment. Thus we can see that people's vital desires are always intertwined with their social and cultural lives.

INTRODUCTION

ENTERING THE WORLD OF NEANDERTHAL MAN

INTRODUCTION

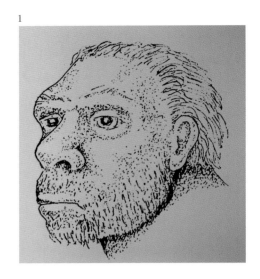

The Neanderthal represents a phase of human evolution that started in Europe, moved to the Near East, and finally went as far as the distant regions of Uzbekistan. The name *Neanderthal* comes from the place in Germany where, in 1856, a top of a skull with a receding forehead was found, along with some skeletal remains. These archaeological finds revealed facial traits that were similar to those of other remains found earlier at Engis

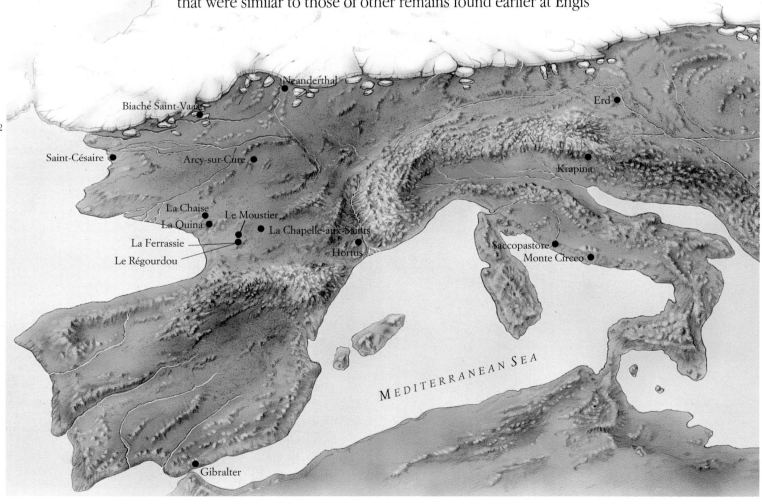

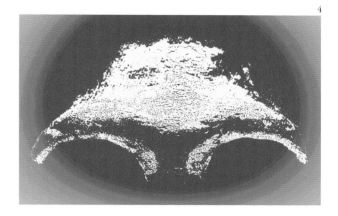

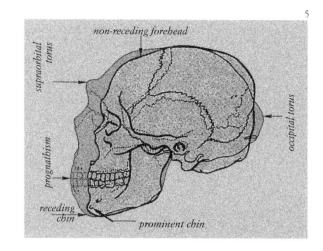

(Belgium) and Gibraltar. Later, there were further discoveries with these same traits: La Chapelle-aux-Saints, La Ferrassie, Le Moustier, Taubach, La Quina, Hortus, Saccopastore, Monte Circeo, etc., all attesting to the presence of this stage of human life in Europe during the first part of the Würm Ice Age (80,000–40,000 years ago.)

The Neanderthal developed from the European pre-Neanderthal who lived during the last interglacial period (Riss-Würm). Pre-Neanderthal comes out of the same family tree as *Homo erectus (Homo heidelbergensis)*, whose remains have been found at Tautavel, Petralona, Bilzingsleben, Steinheim, and other places. *Homo erectus*, who reached Europe about one million years ago, evolved into Neanderthals, strong, stocky humans whose body was well adapted to a cold climate.

1. A reconstruction of the face of a man found at La Chapelle-aux-Saints, Corrèze (France), where a Neanderthal burial was first discovered. This indicates the existence of funeral practices for Neanderthal humans.

2. On the map we see important places in Europe where remains of Homo neanderthalensis *have been found.*

3. On the map we also see some of the places in the Middle East where evidence that has been helpful for research about Neanderthal humans was found.

4. The top of a skull of a Neanderthal human found in a cave in the Neanderthal Valley, near Düsseldorf (Germany). This place gave Neanderthals their name.

5. Two skulls: Homo sapiens neanderthalensis *(in orange) and* Homo sapiens sapiens *(in beige): the profiles show how different the skulls are.*

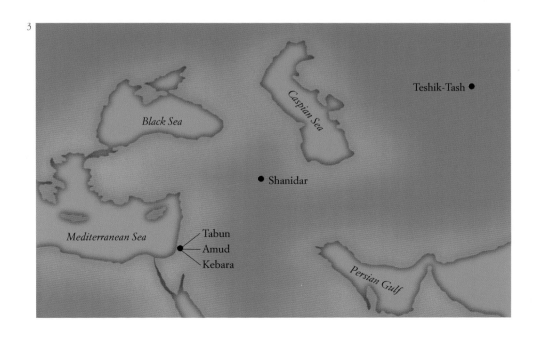

1. The study of the Cave of Hortus, in the town hall of Valflaunès, 16 miles (21 km) north of Montpellier (France) traced the evolution of climate over several thousand years. Neanderthal hunters used this cave in various ways during different climatic periods. In the first drawing, we see a reconstruction of the environment during the cold, humid period, when tall grasses and trees such as pine, oak, and birch, coexisted. During this time, humans only visited the cave occasionally and for short periods.

2. This drawing is a reconstruction of the environment during the time when the weather was warmer but still humid. Grasses gave way to plants that thrive in a wet climate. At this time, humans visited the cave more frequently. During the winter, they participated in more sedentary activities, such as butchering meat.

3. The landscape pictured here shows a period when winters were harsh and summers were fairly hot. The land is steppe-like: many of the trees have disappeared and given way to various species of herbs and rare bushes. During this time, hunters set up temporary summer encampments.

4. The chart summarizes the evolution of the landscape's vegetation in the area of the Cave of Hortus. This study is based on analyses of traces of pollens that were embedded in sediment in the ground.

The Neanderthal is characterized by a continuous supraorbital torus, an occipital torus surmounted by the suprainiac fossa, a massive prominent jaw, and receding forehead. Neanderthal's skull has a cranial capacity larger than that of his predecessors, up to 92–97 cubic inches (1,500–1,600 cc). Other distinct traits include a deep dorsal groove in the scapula and a long, narrow pubic bone. Neanderthal is also rather stocky with a long torso and somewhat short limbs, which is considered beneficial for people living in a harsh climate.

Remains of European pre-Neanderthals from the last inter-glacial period (about 100,000 years ago) have been found in Ehringsdorf, Krapina, La Chaise, Biache Saint-Vaast, Reilingen, Ganovce, and Saccopastore. These specimens appear to have had

1

thousands of years ago	2000	1900	1800	1700	1600	1500	1400	1300	1200	1200	1100	1000	900
Epochs	Pliocene			Lower Pleistocene									
Periods													
Glaciations	Donau			Donau-Günz								Günz	
Climate												First cold wave	
Some Characteristics												Disintegration of forest which gave way to steppe and swamps Great volcanic eruption	
Culture						Pebble Culture							
Cultural Epochs													Low

10

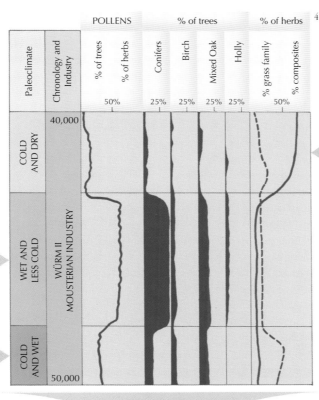

		POLLENS		% of trees				% of herbs	
Paleoclimate	Chronology and Industry	% of trees	% of herbs	Conifers	Birch	Mixed Oak	Holly	% grass family	% composites
		50%		25%	25%	25%	25%	50%	
COLD AND DRY	WÜRM II MOUSTERIAN INDUSTRY	40,000							
WET AND LESS COLD									
COLD AND WET		50,000							

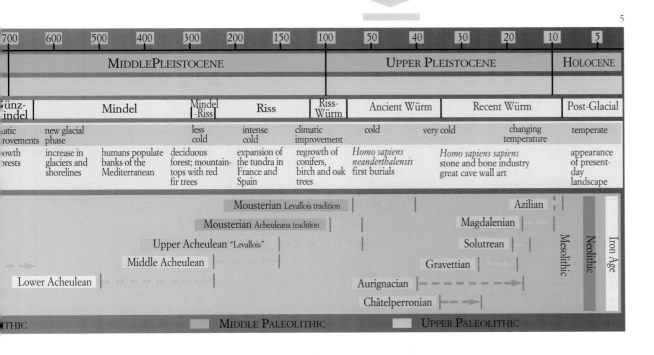

5. A chart of the geological epochs and glaciations, with their climates and cultures, up to the beginning of the Iron Age. The dates are shown in thousands of years. Included here are the climatic conditions that prevailed at the Cave of Hortus.

| 700 | 600 | 500 | 400 | 300 | 200 | 150 | 100 | 50 | 40 | 30 | 20 | 10 | 5 |

| MIDDLE PLEISTOCENE | UPPER PLEISTOCENE | HOLOCENE |

| ünz-indel | Mindel | Mindel-Riss | Riss | Riss-Würm | Ancient Würm | Recent Würm | Post-Glacial |

| atic rovements | new glacial phase | | less cold | intense cold | climatic improvement | cold | very cold | changing temperature | temperate |
| owth rests | increase in glaciers and shorelines | humans populate banks of the Mediterranean | deciduous forest; mountain-tops with red fir trees | expansion of the tundra in France and Spain | regrowth of conifers, birch and oak trees | *Homo sapiens neanderthalensis* first burials | *Homo sapiens sapiens* stone and bone industry great cave wall art | | appearance of present-day landscape |

Mouysterian Levallois tradition

Mousterian Acheuleana tradition

Azilian

Magdalenian

Upper Acheulean "Levallois"

Solutrean

Middle Acheulean

Gravettian

Lower Acheulean

Aurignacian

Châtelperronian

Mesolithic

Neolithic

Iron Age

| THIC | MIDDLE PALEOLITHIC | UPPER PALEOLITHIC |

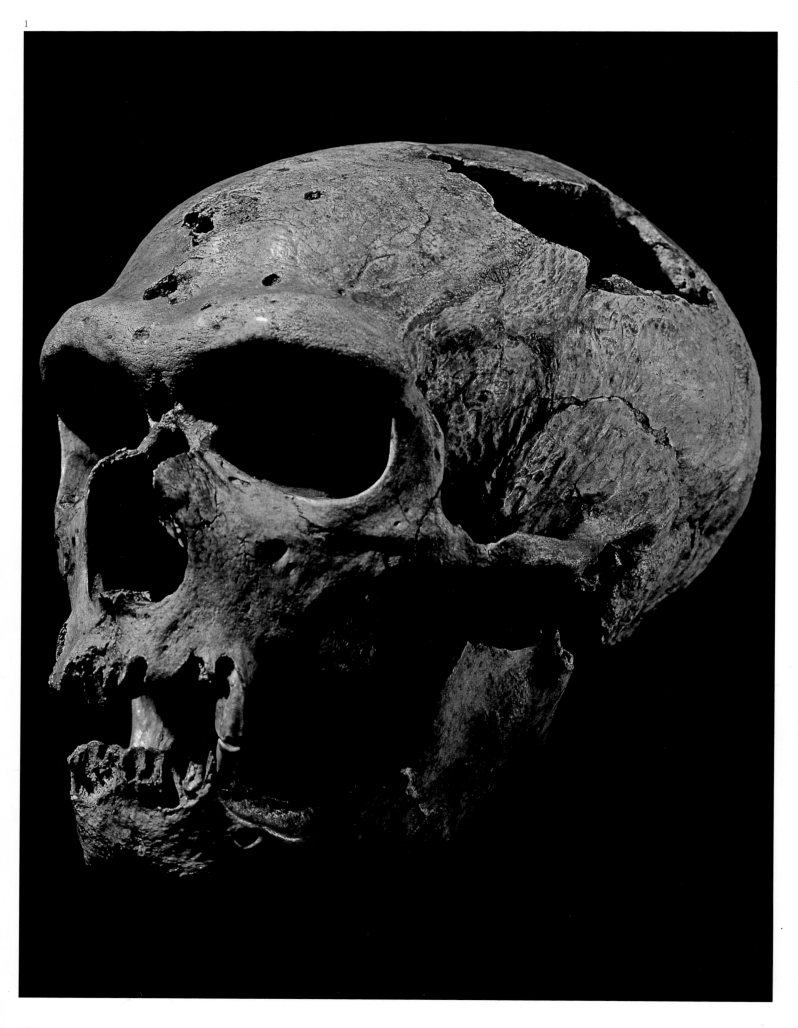

less severe facial features. It is believed that these humans migrated to the Near East where they lived about 90,000–40,000 years ago. Remains of Neanderthals have been found in Tabun, Amud, Kebara (Palestine), Shanidar (Iraq), and Teshik-Tash (Uzbekistan).

The Neanderthals lived in outdoor encampments or in caves or rock shelters where they created living areas with specific purposes. Dwellings made with mammoth bones have even been found.

They hunted animals that lived in a cold climate (reindeer, deer, mammoth, cave bears, marmots, hares, etc.) and made use of their meat, skins, bones, and ivory. The skins were used for clothing and for huts.

1. A skull of a Neanderthal human, discovered in a grave at La Chappelle-aux-Saints (France). The well-preserved skeleton dates from about 60,000 years ago and is typical of a Neanderthal of that period.

2. A chart showing the phylogenetic relationship between European and Middle Eastern fossils. Scientists agree that some Neanderthal humans moved from Europe to the Middle East, and modern humans from the Middle East to Europe.

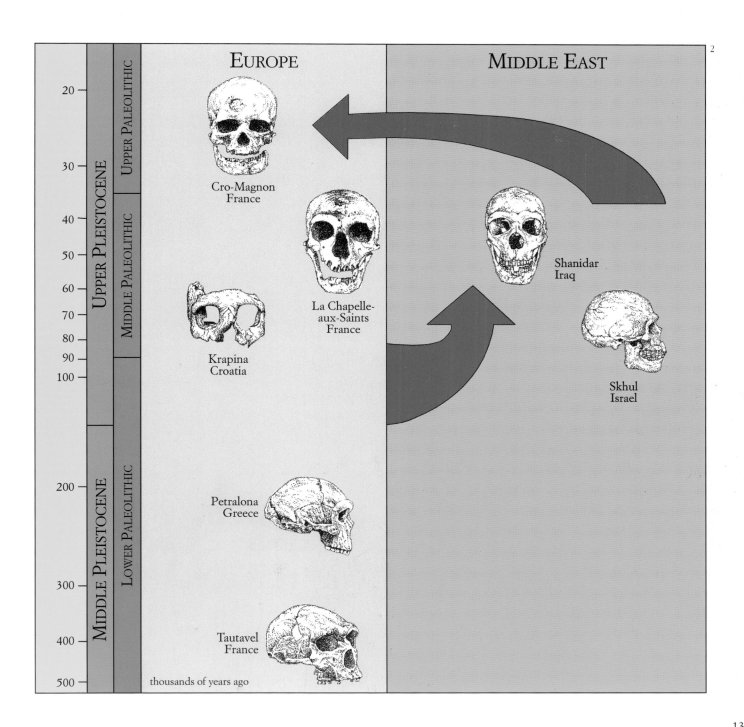

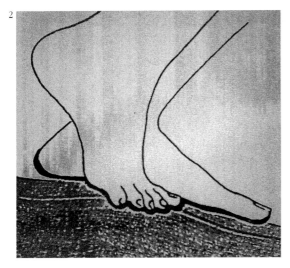

Neanderthals developed techniques for stoneknapping, obtaining bifaces and flake tools. The Levallois technique was used for making stone points, scrapers, and scratchers. The long bones of animals were also used to make tools and daggers. The culture of the classic Neanderthal is called Mousterian.

Neanderthals definitely knew how to use fire, which protected them from the cold and made food easier to consume.

They had nonutilitarian interests, gathering objects such as odd-shaped stones and fossilized shells. We know that they used ochre powder for decoration purposes. They also carved bones. Some long animal bones appear to be musical instruments because of the small holes carved in them.

In Shanidar (Iraq) there have been discoveries of Neanderthal burials in which the corpse was set out on a bed of flowers. In

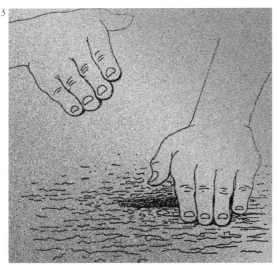

1. In the drawing we see the technique of scratching a deer antler with a flaked flint point. Neanderthal artisans used materials such as bone, horn, and animal teeth, in addition to stone. In order to better understand what they are looking at, scientists measure the amount of "wear and tear" on the objects they find. They try to replicate the sequence of motions that a prehistoric man may have used on a particular material. They find the marks of wear and tear on the object and analyze them under an electronic microscope. By doing this, they can determine which marks on the evidence were caused by nature and which were man-made.

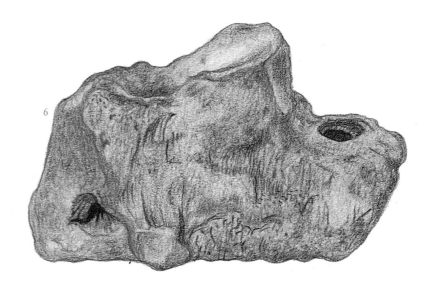

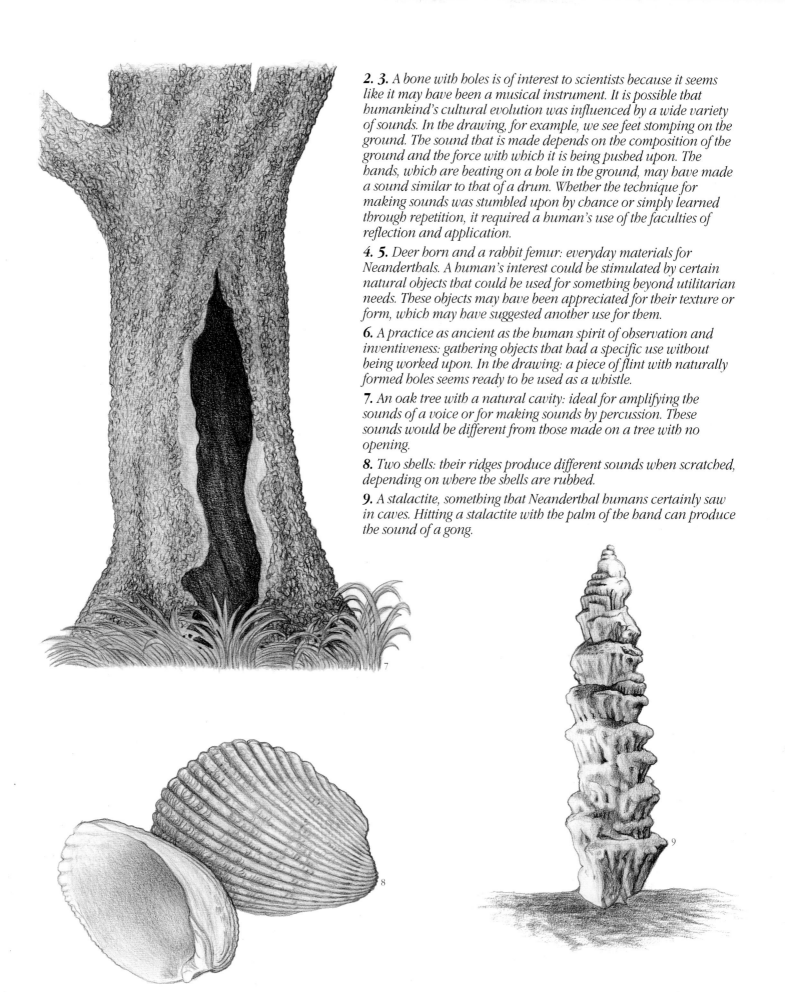

2. 3. A bone with holes is of interest to scientists because it seems like it may have been a musical instrument. It is possible that humankind's cultural evolution was influenced by a wide variety of sounds. In the drawing, for example, we see feet stomping on the ground. The sound that is made depends on the composition of the ground and the force with which it is being pushed upon. The hands, which are beating on a hole in the ground, may have made a sound similar to that of a drum. Whether the technique for making sounds was stumbled upon by chance or simply learned through repetition, it required a human's use of the faculties of reflection and application.

4. 5. Deer horn and a rabbit femur: everyday materials for Neanderthals. A human's interest could be stimulated by certain natural objects that could be used for something beyond utilitarian needs. These objects may have been appreciated for their texture or form, which may have suggested another use for them.

6. A practice as ancient as the human spirit of observation and inventiveness: gathering objects that had a specific use without being worked upon. In the drawing: a piece of flint with naturally formed holes seems ready to be used as a whistle.

7. An oak tree with a natural cavity: ideal for amplifying the sounds of a voice or for making sounds by percussion. These sounds would be different from those made on a tree with no opening.

8. Two shells: their ridges produce different sounds when scratched, depending on where the shells are rubbed.

9. A stalactite, something that Neanderthal humans certainly saw in caves. Hitting a stalactite with the palm of the hand can produce the sound of a gong.

Krapina (Croatia) human broken bones were found, which may indicate cannibalism. The bones may have been broken to remove the marrow. This may have been some kind of ritual.

The last Neanderthals lived in Saint-Césaire (France) about 37,000 years ago and made use of the industrial techniques of Châtelperronian. This was at the same time that modern man (*Homo sapiens sapiens*) arrived from the Near East and brought with him a more advanced culture (Aurignacian). Neanderthal and *Homo sapiens sapiens* must have coexisted for a short time, perhaps peacefully. It is also possible that the two groups may have had genetic breeding with each other. Probably, however, the Neanderthals made little or no contribution to the population of Europe during this period of coexistence.

1. *Yarrow, an herb found with other herbs in a Neanderthal grave in Shanidar (Iraq). Since ancient times, yarrow has been known for its therapeutic qualities. It helps wounds to heal quickly.*

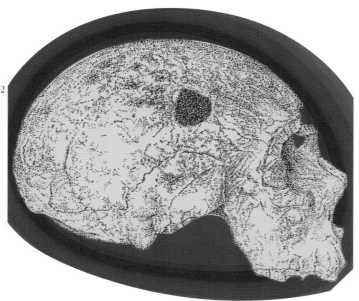

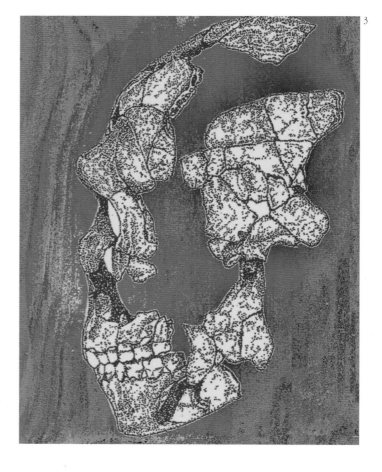

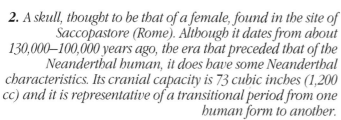

2. *A skull, thought to be that of a female, found in the site of Saccopastore (Rome). Although it dates from about 130,000–100,000 years ago, the era that preceded that of the Neanderthal human, it does have some Neanderthal characteristics. Its cranial capacity is 73 cubic inches (1,200 cc) and it is representative of a transitional period from one human form to another.*

3. *The skull from Saint-Césaire, found in the region of Charente-Maritime (France) dates from 36,000 years ago and is a typical Neanderthal specimen. At the time that this human lived,* Homo sapiens sapiens *was also present in Europe. We now know that at least some Neanderthals disappeared much later than originally believed.*

It is thought that the Neanderthals died out without descendants. This was not necessarily because they were massacred or eliminated in a violent way by other humans. There is a theory that they were not able to resist the germs brought in by the newly arriving population. Or perhaps the cultural superiority of the new arrivals was the reason for the Neanderthals' extinction.

4. *The so-called Skull of Galilee, found at El-Zuttiyeh, shows a mixture of primitive and more evolved traits. It is 150,000 years old and has a cranial capacity of 85 cubic inches (1,400 cc). What is interesting about this skull is that some of its traits are like those of the Neanderthal human, but others are like those of Homo erectus and Homo sapiens. Thus we can see that the boundaries between the different stages of human development are not always clear. Because new evidence from earlier or later eras is still being discovered, unanswered questions remain.*

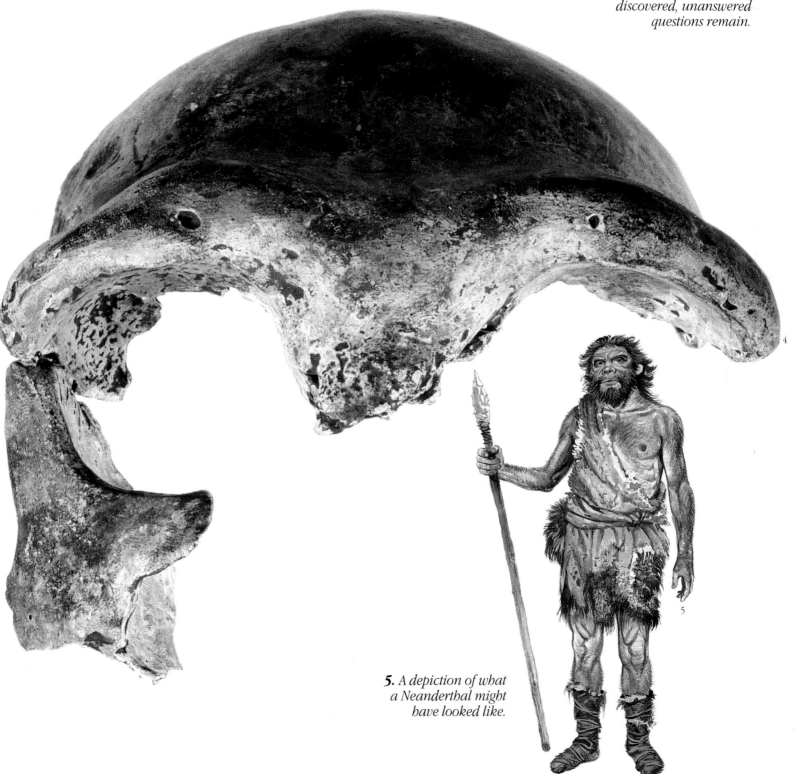

5. *A depiction of what a Neanderthal might have looked like.*

KAWAK'S DAY

DANGER IN THE FOREST

His name is "Kawak," but he is called "The Great One." Right now, he is leading a group deep into the forest where they hope to find a herd of deer.

There are four other men and some young boys with Kawak. They walk among the tall grasses, bushes, and trees. The grasses have already turned yellow, and the tips of the stalks bear ears. Rubbing them between their fingers, the men are able to obtain a few grains, which they eat with gusto.

They continue out to a plain where two valleys meet. "There," says Kawak, "we will find animals drinking."

They walk with difficulty and Kawak advises them, "Be careful where you step because there could be snakes hidden in the grass."

Just as he says this, one of the younger boys feels a bite on his foot.

Kawak draws near and sucks the bite in order to spit out the venom. "Now we have to find a plant with large leaves and place it on the wound. It will absorb any poison that is still in there."

1. Fossil from a Neanderthal human's possible prey: the giant deer (Megalocerus giganteus), whose head and antlers could be as large as 7 feet (2 m) across.

2. 3. The drawings show the skull of a poisonous snake with its mouth open and closed. If the mouth is open, the poisonous fang is vertical and ready to give off a dangerous substance. Neanderthal hunters were sometimes victims of this tremendous mechanism.

4. Neanderthal humans learned the healing power of certain plants. In the photo we see horsetail (Equisetum arvense). This plant, which was found in the midst of other flowers and medicinal herbs in the Neanderthal grave at Shanidar (Iraq), can disinfect, clot blood, and close up a wound.

5. The diagram shows the growth patterns of the antlers of two animals from Neanderthal times: on the right, the red deer (Cervus elaphus); and on the left, a fallow deer (Dama dama). Studying these stages of growth in remains has been useful in determining what seasons were best for hunting.

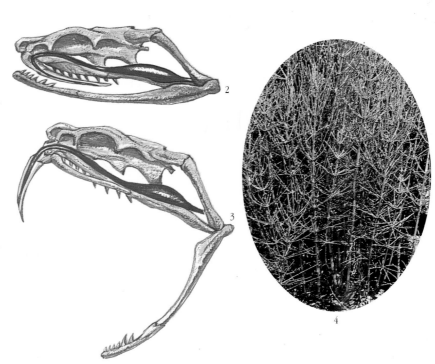

years 2 3 4 5 6 7 years 2 3 4 5 6

KOS

Kawak's group is coming close to its destination. The young boys are sad and speak of their younger brother, Kos, who died yesterday.

"Kos was a good boy. He ate something poisonous, and he started to throw up. He died quickly."

Kawak says: "We will bury him when we get back to the cave. Kos is about to start a new life with those who have passed on before him. We want to bury him with some things that will go with him to the next life. We will bury him with part of a deer that we will catch. It will be our offering."

Just as Kawak finishes speaking, a herd of deer approach a stream to drink. This is the moment the men have been waiting for. The youngest boys spread out so that they can corner the deer in the valley. The others will attack the deer with spears and stones.

1. A skull found at a site in Krapina (Croatia). The arrow points to different, future ways of honoring the dead.

2. A sculptured elk head from a double grave at Oleniy Ostrov (Deer Island), on Lake Onega (Russia), late sixth–early fifth millennium B.C.E.

3. 4. A tomb in the cemetery of Kheit Qasim (Iraq), 2850–2800 B.C.E., with bowls that indicate a funeral feast during which food was placed near the corpse. To the right: a ceramic fragment found in the grave, painted with designs of goats, a symbol of society.

5. A bowl painted by the Mimbres Indians (A.D. 1000–1200), a vanished people of the American Southwest. The dead person was given items like this to take to the underworld. The bowl, made by women and linked to an ancient story about conserving and cooking food, was punched before being placed in the grave. The object was symbolically "killed" so it could accompany the deceased.

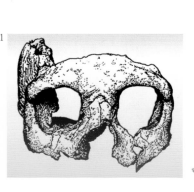

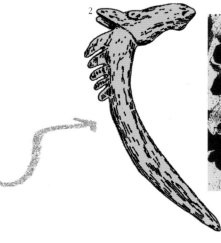

5

6. *Mandible of a Neanderthal human, found at La Ferrassie, in the Dordogne (France). Study under the microscope of the recognizable wear and tear marks on the teeth tells us something about the eating habits of prehistoric humans. Based on what is seen, the human diet was probably rather varied and tough.*

6

1

1. We can see the grandeur of the skeleton of this giant deer, which lived during the Pleistocene period. Our arrow points to some representations of this animal in prehistoric art. The deer was important as a source of food and useful, workable material.

2. A rock painting (6000–3500 B.C.E.) discovered in Catalonia (Spain) and now housed in the Barcelona Museum. It shows a deer of great proportions.

3. This work (3200–2500 B.C.E.) was carved on a boulder in Val Camonica (Italy): a supernatural being with a solar disk face; five daggers, emblem of strength; a river belt, symbol of life and death; and finally, a deer, which ensures unity between humans and nature.

4. From the pre-Columbian Cospi codex (1350–1500 C.E.), housed in the Central University Library in Bologna (Italy): a deer next to a divinity represents a day in the ritual calendar when rites of conservation of the most hunted animals are celebrated. The codex is made of deer hide.

5. The head of a marmot, a rodent that hides in dens that it builds underground.

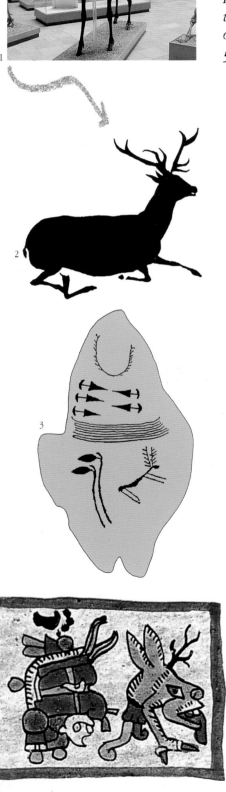

2

3

4

5

THE DEER HUNT

The deer are drinking from the stream. The men hope that one of them will be cornered or will catch its antlers in the bushes or trees as it tries to run away.

One of them does run away from the attackers but stops as it enters the forest. The forest is very thick, and the deer's antlers get stuck in some branches. It cannot get away. The men are able to attack it with their spears and sticks.

They tie its legs to a pole, and two men carry it. They take the shortest route back to the cave.

On the way back, one of the boys points out holes in the ground that he has noticed.

Kawak explains: "Those lead to the dens of an animal who burrows underground [the marmot]. He is a nice little animal. Whenever you hear a long whistle, it means that this animal is sending a signal to another one of his species. He may be warning them of some danger or transmitting a message that we cannot understand."

A SURPRISE AT HOME

The men are returning to the cave a different way. They walk along a rocky ridge, which, according to Kawak, may present something interesting.

The sun is still fairly high on the horizon. When it starts to set, they reach the foot of a large cliff that is partially hidden by fir trees, acacia trees, and bushes.

"Pay attention," says Kawak. "Look among the rocks that have fallen from the hill. You may find some that are sparkling or are colorful."

And so the group begins its search. In a little while, one of the boys shouts, "Look, I found a green stone!" [serpentine]. Then another one shouts, "Here is a transparent stone that is very hard and smooth [quartz]. Let's bring these treasures to Mother."

Another boy, who has wandered off from the group, returns, panting, with two rather heavy stones that are shiny golden-brown [pyrite].

"It is a very beautiful mineral," says Kawak, "and it can be used to make a fire."

And with that, Kawak strikes one piece of stone against another above some dry twigs. Sparks fly and set the twigs on fire.

1

2

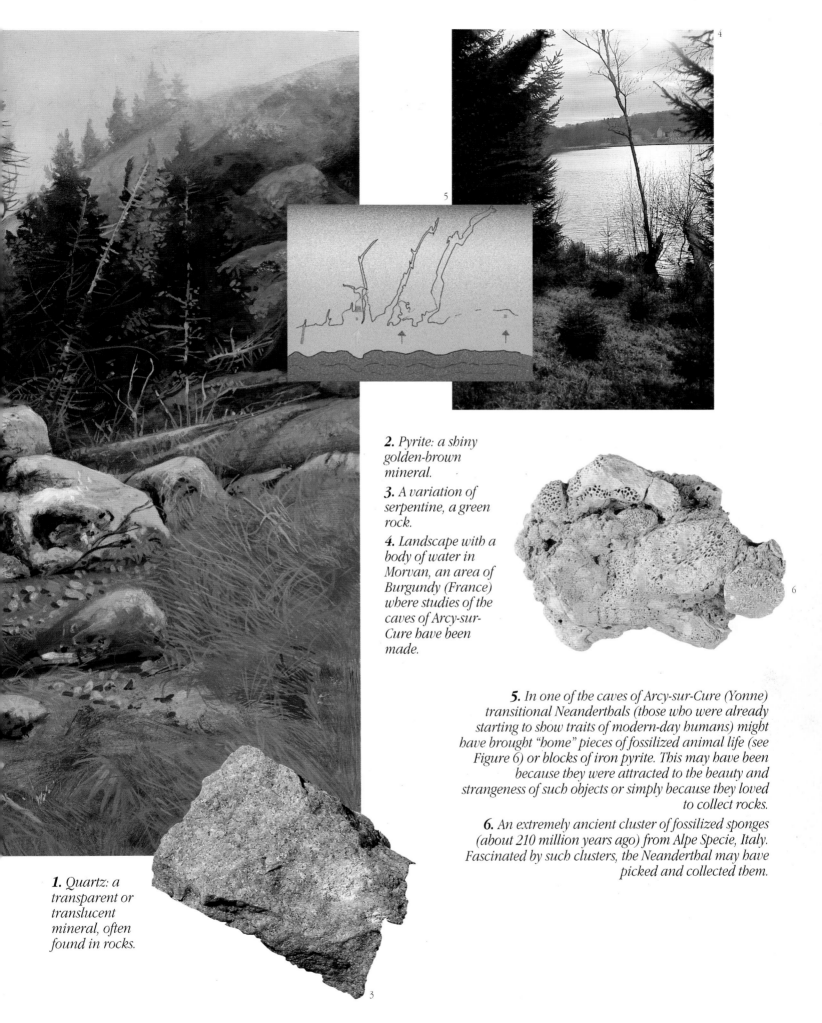

2. *Pyrite: a shiny golden-brown mineral.*

3. *A variation of serpentine, a green rock.*

4. *Landscape with a body of water in Morvan, an area of Burgundy (France) where studies of the caves of Arcy-sur-Cure have been made.*

5. *In one of the caves of Arcy-sur-Cure (Yonne) transitional Neanderthals (those who were already starting to show traits of modern-day humans) might have brought "home" pieces of fossilized animal life (see Figure 6) or blocks of iron pyrite. This may have been because they were attracted to the beauty and strangeness of such objects or simply because they loved to collect rocks.*

6. *An extremely ancient cluster of fossilized sponges (about 210 million years ago) from Alpe Specie, Italy. Fascinated by such clusters, the Neanderthal may have picked and collected them.*

1. *Quartz: a transparent or translucent mineral, often found in rocks.*

27

A LITTLE WORKSHOP

The way home is short. Not far from the cave where they live, the men come to another place where some of the men from their group are working on flints.

It is a little workshop that has been set up under a rock shelter where there is plenty of brown-colored stone that is well suited to flaking.

Kawak observes with satisfaction the tools that have already been worked. There are points, scrapers, scratchers, and knives. Next to these are the attempted projects that did not succeed. They are the waste material of the workshop.

Murial is an excellent artisan and is demonstrating how to make different tools. The nucleus of stone can be hit with another stone, or it can be placed on a hard surface and hit with a hammer.

1. A rock shelter would have been useful for Neanderthals' needs. In the photo: a rocky cliff in the forest of Derborence (Switzerland).

2. Example of a flaked point from Saccopastore (Rome).

3. We can see how a scraper found at Monte Circeo, near Rome, looked. The tool is made by chipping away angular pieces at the top and along both of the edges of a rounded stone flake. Such tools were plentiful during the recent Paleolithic age, but were also made before that.

4. *A scratcher, from Erd (Hungary). This is different from a scraper because it is usually flaked and retouched on only one edge of the stone.*

5. *A knife found in Arcy-sur-Cure. The drawing shows how there may have been a handle (outlined in red) on one of the two sides.*

A CLEVER TECHNIQUE

1. *Modern experimental replica of a tool associated with Neanderthal humans: a nucleus of stone from which a flake has been obtained, using the Levallois technique. The name Levallois comes from the site near Paris where use of the technique was first discovered.*

2. *A scratcher, also made with the Levallois technique.*

3. 4. *Levallois points.*

5. *The drawing shows several stages of Levallois work done on a nucleus of stone. On the yellow background: the gradual removal of the outer surface of the nucleus, the cortex. On the blue background: the nucleus from which the flake was obtained and the flake itself. We can see that at the end of the process, the flake has turned out as originally planned.*

6. 7. *Two different ways of retouching a flake of stone. Below: the flake is held in the hand and worked with a wooden hammer. Above: the flake is held on an anvil, allowing the hammer to have a stronger effect.*

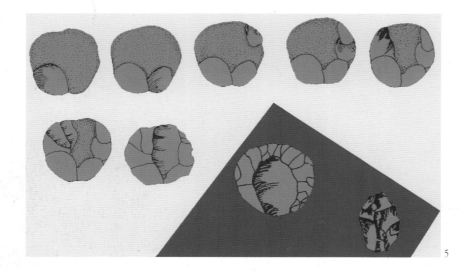

We are still in the little workshop where the men use flint to make tools.

A special technique that Murial wants to teach the younger boys is one that uses a core of stone [Levallois technique]. The shape of the tool that will be made is decided upon first, by means of striking off flakes around the core. Then the core is struck along the edge and a blade is produced. This is a good way to get the greatest number of tools from one piece of stone.

Murial has shown great skill in flint flaking. Now Murial shows how to obtain finer tools from the stone. All one has to do is refine a flake with a soft hammer that is made from deer antler and the edge of the flake becomes sharp and denticulated. This beautiful tool will be useful for cutting meat or skinning animals.

THE CAVE DWELLING

The men in our group have now reached the cave that lies under a hillside. This is where they live.

While some of them bring the deer to the place where it will be butchered, Kawak stands at the opening of the cave, greets his wife, Anel, and tells her of the day's events.

Anel is working on some animal skins that will be clothes for the children. The children have gone off to gather flowers that they will put into the grave with Kos.

Kawak passes by a curtain made from animal skin that separates the open area of the cave from the inner area. He goes inside.

On one side, set in a cubbyhole, the skull of a bear seems to watch over and protect the little family.

Kawak rests for a moment while Anel fixes him something to drink. Then he says, "We must make a meal that we will eat in memory of Kos. Then we will take his lifeless body to the cave where we will bury it."

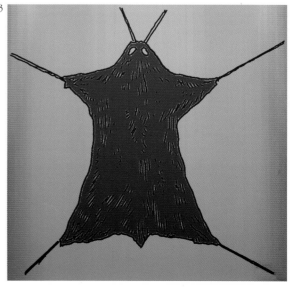

1. Artist's conception of the Neanderthal site of Le Moustier, in the Dordogne (France). From an engraving of the second half of the nineteenth century.

2. The skull of Ursus spelaeus *(a cave bear) dating from the Pleistocene period. It was found in northern Italy.*

3. The drawing shows an animal skin that has been stretched out to dry. Working on animal skins was one of the skills acquired by prehistoric humans in their effort to make use of every part of the animal they had killed.

4. A sprig of broom (Spartium junceum). Broom can grow several meters high. Its bright yellow flowers are hard to miss. Neanderthal humans placed these flowers in graves.

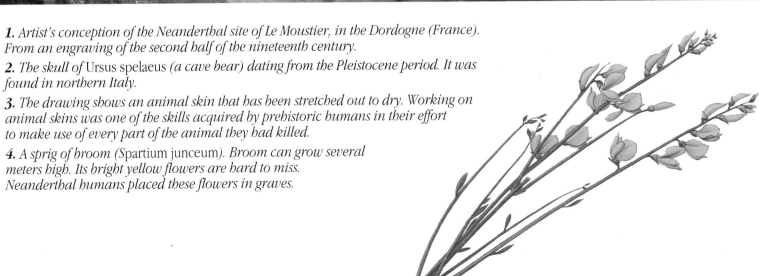

4

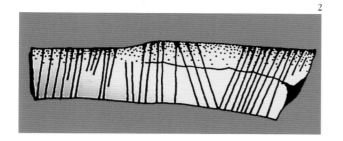

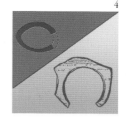

A GIFT FOR MOTHER

While Kawak and Anel are still at home, two boys arrive: the one who had found the shiny stone; the other, who is holding the very hard stone that is a shiny golden-brown. Both of them are bringing these stones to their mother because they think she will be pleased. Mother thanks the boys and places the stones in a cubbyhole near some others.

Kawak comments, "The shiny green stone helps to beautify our home. The other one will help us to light a fire."

Kawak and Anel leave the cave. They see one of their sons, Krabu, who is carving a design on the antler of a deer.

"What are you doing?" Kawak asks Krabu.

"I am drawing the path that we took to get to the valley where the deer were. This way, we will know how to get back the next time."

Meanwhile, the children who were gathering flowers return. They have found broom and acacia flowers for Kos's grave.

1. *A fragment of a long, carved bone dating from more than 47,000 years ago was found in the Cave Băčo Kiro (Bulgaria). Its zigzag design was made by the repetitive movements of an engraving tool. According to scientists, the repetitive design is undoubtedly deliberate.*

2. *A bone fragment carved with parallel lines, found in the site of La Ferrassie, in the Dordogne (France).*

3. *An awl found in the Reindeer Cave at Arcy-sur-Cure (France).*

4. *Also found in the same cave, a blade made of bone that has been cut along its curve. Although we know that ancient humans worked on bone and ivory, we still do not know of a systematic method that they used. We do know that bone, with its nutritious marrow, was more than just a source of food.*

THE MAMMOTH

The fire is being prepared for roasting the deer. It has been cut in four pieces. The stomach and the intestines have been put aside. The pieces of deer have been laid out on two stones, and between the two stones a fire has been lit.

All of a sudden a cloud of dust is seen at the foot of the hill. A trumpeting sound is heard: It is a herd of mammoth passing by.

"It's the curved-tusked elephants!" exclaims Kawak. "This means that the cold season is approaching and we will have to look for a better place to live. These are the first mammoths to pass by here. They are difficult to catch. They sometimes fall into a trap after we drive them toward a swamp or cliff. Once they are in a difficult position or are wounded, it is easier to stab them with spears. They are very useful animals. We need them for their meat as well as their tusks and fur."

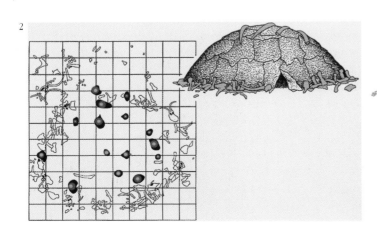

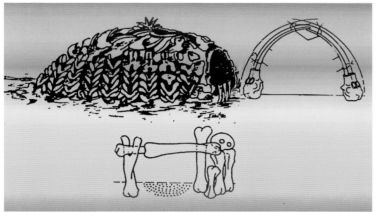

1. Museum visitors observe a mammoth skeleton.

2. From the 44,000-year-old hut made of mammoth bones, discovered in Moldova (Ukraine), the arrow shows us how the mammoth stimulated human creativity over time.

3. At the foot of the Pavlov Mountains in the Czech Republic, where the Dolní Věstonice site is (29,000-25,000 B.C.E.), a clay statue of a stylized mammoth was found.

4. Elegant and elaborate mammoth bone huts (17,800–14,300 B.C.E.) have been found at Mezhirich (Ukraine). This one had a spit and painted mammoth bones and skulls.

THE FUNERAL FEAST

This is the last meal with Kos. His lifeless body has been laid out on the meadow, a short distance away. He is in a sleeping position.

The deer meat will be eaten in his honor, with his body nearby. The deer has been skinned, and its meat, which has been roasted on the fire, is now ready to be eaten. The deer's skin has been set aside. It will be used for making clothing.

Seated around the fire are Kawak, his wife, Anel, the children, and the other men and women of the group.

Kim, the youngest child, turns to his mother and asks, "Why is Kos cold, and why does he not speak or move?"

"Because he is dead," Mother replies.

"And why did he die? Wouldn't it be nice if we could be all together?"

Kawak answers: "You see, Kim, before us, there lived others who are no longer alive, like my parents, our ancestors. One day we too will die and others will take our place. But everything has not ended for those who have passed on before us. Now they are on a long journey, and we will accompany them in our thoughts. Kos is beginning his journey. This is why we will gather around his body and honor him. To see him off as he leaves for his new life, we will bury him with the head of this deer that we are eating and some small tools. And we will cover his body with red ochre powder, a symbol of life and death."

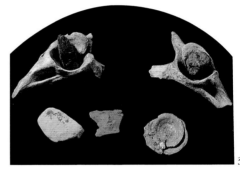

1. Ochre played a role in prehistory. This colorful material was symbolic, and, perhaps because its red color was reminiscent of blood, it was used in ancient rites and in art. The arrow shows its use over time.

2. Ornamental and decorative objects were found in a cave at Arcy-sur-Cure (France). In the photo: an ochre deposit from the recent Paleolithic age.

3. Some of the most beautiful prehistoric pictures have been discovered in the Altamira Cave (Spain), about 18,000-13,000 B.C.E. In the photo: remains of ochre in containers made from shells and vertebrae. Coal has also been found. These may have been artists' materials.

4. A mammoth bone decorated with ochre found in Mezin (Ukraine), dating from about 15,000 years ago.

The meal is over, and now it is time to bring Kos's body to the pit where he will be buried, near the cave.

Some of the members of the group take a stretcher and lay the corpse on it. Kawak carries the deer's head by the antlers.

The children are holding some tools. Mother and the other women carry flowers.

1. *A stone slab covering a grave at La Ferrassie, in the Dordogne (France) where various Neanderthal burials were discovered. According to scientists, the small holes might have been made by Neanderthals.*

2. *A Neanderthal skull, which appears to have been left in its original state, was found in a cave at Monte Circeo (Rome). In the drawing we see it as it was at the moment it was discovered, surrounded by a circle of stones. The skull reveals some kind of mutilation, which could be evidence of ritual cannibalism, performed in order to take possession of the deceased person's vital energy. Recent studies reject this interpretation.*

The grave is ready. The flowers are strewn about to make a kind of bed upon which to lay the body. Kos is then placed in the grave. The deer's head is placed next to Kos's head, and the children place the tools around him.

Kawak sprinkles the red powder on the body and says, "May you live a new life!" Then he throws a handful of earth onto Kos's body. The others do the same. Each person lays a flower in the grave.

Their wish is that Kos will thrive in his new life.

3. *In Le Régourdou (France), there is Europe's oldest burial: a Neanderthal human under a pile of stones (in the drawing, in orange). Next to him, covered by a slab of stone, are the remains of a bear (in the drawing, in gray). The relationship between the two structures is unknown.*

4. *A Neanderthal skeleton dating from 60,000 years ago was discovered in a cave at Kebara (Israel). Its skull had been removed without disturbing the rest of the body. This may have been part of an unknown rite.*

5. *A Neanderthal child buried at Teshik-Tash (Uzbekistan): the remains of the skull are surrounded by ibex horns.*

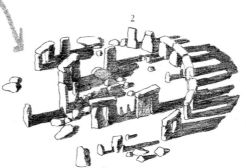

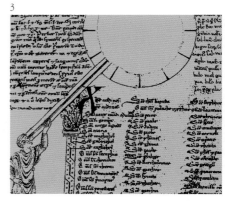

THE DAY ENDS

A fire has been lit in front of the cave, and the men, women, and children are seated around it. The leftovers from the meal have been buried in a nearby pit. Now, before retiring for the night, the members of the group exchange their thoughts about the day.

"It has been a sad day because from now on Kos will no longer be with us."

"Yes, but Kos is still close to us," Kawak comments, "even if we do not know where the Great Spirit has brought him."

Then there is a moment of silence, and Kawak speaks again. "Soon we will have to leave this place. The harsh season is coming, and the snow will force us to look for a warmer place. Do you notice that the sun is lower in the sky, and so it produces less heat? This means the cold season is drawing near."

One of the children interrupts, "And the moon gets smaller and smaller. . . ."

"Yes, but that means something else. The moon gets smaller and smaller, but then it starts to grow again; it gets bigger, then it gets smaller, it disappears and reappears. And this goes on all the time."

"And the stars?" asks the same child.

"For the stars, things are different," observes Kawak. "Some keep their places in the sky, others change. If you really look hard, you will see that some stars are arranged in the shape of an animal: a lion, a bull, a scorpion . . . those stars shine every night with him who is up in heaven so that we do not feel alone."

1. *The galaxy Andromeda, which can be seen by the naked eye on clear nights. The arrow points to mysteries of the sky that attracted humans over time and served as inspiration for poetry and knowledge.*

2. *At Stonehenge (England), there is an imposing structure built between 3000 and 1500 B.C.E. The drawing shows enormous rocks fixed in the ground in concentric circles. Stonehenge may have been an observatory or a temple to the sun.*

3. *A monk surveys the sky with a telescope (from a codex of St. Gallen's Abbey, Switzerland, dating from around the year 1000 C.E.). Studying the heavens was part of monastic life.*

4. *The ancient Peking observatory (seventeenth century). According to the traditions of Chinese science, observing the stars can give one a vision of the universe.*

GLOSSARY

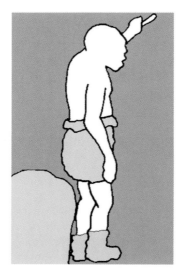

A Neanderthal lookout on a hilltop is pointing out animals on the horizon. Hunting was an activity organized to ensure the survival of families.

AURIGNACIAN: An Upper Paleolithic culture linked to modern humans. The name comes from the Cave of Aurignac in the northern Garonne (France).

BIFACE: A stone tool, typical of the Paleolithic period, in various shapes: pear, almond, heart, oval, etc. It is flaked, and eventually retouched, on both faces and along the edges.

COMPOSITES (scientific name COMPOSITE or ASTERACEAE): A widespread family of herbs, including about 20,000 species, in which the florets are borne in a close head, as the daisy.

CRANIAL CAPACITY: Volume of the braincase. It is measured in cubic centimeters.

CULTURE: In the field of prehistory, the ability to modify nature intentionally, to control or transform the environment, to acquire and transmit knowledge, to know how to benefit from experience, and to express one's own internal world beyond the needs of everyday life.

DENTICULATED: Denoting an object whose edges are jagged.

EVOLUTION: The gradual transformation of species of animals or plants.

EXTINCTION: The complete disappearance from the realm of living beings.

FLAKE: Roughly short and wide tool obtained from a nucleus of stone by percussion.

FLINT: Sedimentary rock formed by the accumulation of various types of deposits. It was very useful in prehistoric tool making because of its fine grain and hardness.

FOSSIL: From the Latin word meaning "to dig." One actually needs to dig to find fossils, which are evidence of ancient living organisms preserved in layers of rock. Traces of prehistoric human activity, such as deposits of stones or

Caring for children was and still is an important way to transfer culture.

bones, artifacts, imprints and footprints, all belong to the world of fossils.

FOSSILIZATION: A natural process of preservation made possible by the coming together of various favorable circumstances and phenomena linked to the nature of the organism and environmental conditions.

GLACIATION: Cold geological period characterized by vast extensions of ice in regions of the northern hemisphere.

GRASS FAMILY (scientific name GRAMINAE or POACEAE): A widespread family of herbs, including about 8,000 species, with jointed stems, sheathing leaves, and seedlike fruits. Well known are the cereals such as rice, wheat, and corn.

HAMMER: Stone tool, chosen for its shape and resistance, used to strike sharply a nucleus in order to detach a flake from it. (See also PERCUSSION).

HOLOCENE: The geologic period following the glaciations, which encompasses the last 10,000 years.

HOMO ERECTUS: The type of human who lived between 1.6 million and 150,000 years ago.

The first step in making a specific tool from stone is to choose suitable pieces of stone.

HOMO SAPIENS: A human more evolved than *Homo erectus*. There were three forms of *Homo Sapiens* linked with evidence that has been found dating from 100,000 to 10,000 years ago: the very ancient and extinct *Homo sapiens antiquus;* a more specialized but also extinct *Homo sapiens neanderthalensis;* and finally, one who is not different from humans as we know them today, *Homo sapiens sapiens.*

INDUSTRY (PREHISTORIC): Items that early humans made from flint, bone, and horn that had an intentional use.

INTERGLACIAL PERIOD: A time period that falls between two glaciations, with a less severe, warmer climate.

LAYER: In zoology, each manifestation of the male deer's antlers.

The layers of a deer's antlers could be scraped and saved for making hammers. Deer lose their antlers in the autumn but grow new ones in the spring. This cycle of life's renewal may have been the reason that humans used the deer as a symbol of so many aspects of life.

MOUSTERIAN: A Middle Paleolithic culture that takes its name from the site at Le Moustier, the Dordogne (France).

NEOLITHIC: Later Stone Age, which falls between the tenth and fourth millennia B.C.E. This age witnessed the beginning of agriculture, breeding, the production of ceramics, and the first permanent villages.

NUCLEUS (or CORE): Block of stone from which many kinds of tools are made.

OCCIPITAL BONE: A flat bone located in the back of the skull.

PALEOLITHIC: Early Stone Age (700,000 to 10,000 years ago). Scientists divide it into three parts. The Lower Paleolithic took place 700,000 to 120,000 years ago. The presence of *Homo erectus* covers this entire time span, but it actually begins much earlier, 1.6 million years ago, in the Archeolithic era, which is characterized by Oldowan industry (choppers and chopping tools). The Middle Paleolithic took place 120,000 to 40,000 years ago, and the Upper Paleolithic took place 40,000 to 10,000 years ago.

Neanderthals butchering a mammoth. Some of the meat will be brought back to the encampment. The rest of it will be buried in the snow to keep for later use.

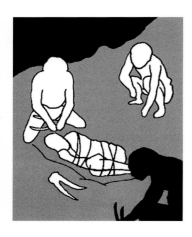

Humans created important funeral rites and gave special attention to caring for the deceased. Neanderthals have left behind many graves that testify to their ability to be concerned with something beyond their everyday, immediate needs. Graves also tell us something about the Neanderthals' high level of cultural and spiritual life.

PERCUSSION: A strong blow with which a nucleus of stone is being hit to break off a flake. This can be done *directly* with a stone or horn hammer, or *indirectly* by putting another stone between the nucleus and the hammer, or even with *pressure* from a tool called a retoucher.

PHYLOGENETIC: Concerning the evolution of a particular group of organisms.

PLEISTOCENE: Period of the Quaternary era characterized by glaciations. It began 1.8 million years ago and continued until 10,000 years ago.

POINTS: Generally small stone tools with a sharp end, worked out from splinters or blades.

POLLEN: The male element in granular form for the sexual reproduction of plants. The outer part is so resistant that it can be conserved in rocky sediments for millions of years and can be studied in the science called palynology.

QUATERNARY: Geological era that began 1.8 million years ago. It includes the Pleistocene and the Holocene periods.

RITE: An individual or group repeated act charged with symbolic references, sometimes to realities beyond this world.

SCAPULA: Either of two flat, triangular bones, each forming the back part of the shoulder.

SEDIMENT: An accumulation of mineral substances in the ground that have undergone a series of changes that have brought about the formation of various deposits and rock.

SITE: Place where remains of prehistoric human and their activities have been found. Such remains, discovered by scientists during a series of archaeological excavations, are then passed on to the next stage of research.

SUPRAINIAC FOSSA: A small concave indentation above the inion, the small external occipital protuberance.

TORUS: Strong protrusion of bone. The "supraorbital torus," or visor, refers to the browridge. The "occipital torus" refers to the occipital bone in the back of the skull.

The tools that Neanderthals made were mostly used for their basic activity, hunting. They were also used for splitting bones to extract the marrow, which was a precious food.

A Neanderthal man observes the surrounding landscape. He and his group set up temporary encampments that they returned to now and again. They had to know the territory very well, memorizing where the rivers and caves were. To do this, they carved marks and lines on bones and stones.

INDEX

Page numbers in *italics* refer to illustrations.

Alpe Specie, Italy, 27
Altamira Cave, Spain, 39
Andromeda galaxy, *42*, 43
Animals, 13, 20, *20*, 22, *24*, 24, 25, 36, *36–37*
Antlers, 20, *21*
Arcy-sur-Cure, France, 27, 29, 35, 39
Aurignacian culture, 16

Bifaces, 14
Broom (*Spartium junceum*), *33*, 33, 35

Cannibalism, 16, 40
Catalonia, Spain, 24
Cave Baco Kiro, Bulgaria, 35
Cave of Hortus, Valflaunès, France, 10, *10*
Châtelperronian, industrial techniques of, 16
Cospi codex, 24

Deer, 20, *20*, 22, 24, *24*, 25
Deer Island, Lake Onega, Russia, 22
Derborence, Switzerland, 28
Dwellings, 13, 32, *32–33*

Engis, Belgium, 8–9
Erd, Hungary, 29

Fire, use of, 14, 26
Flaking, 28, 30, 31
Flints, 28, 31
Food, 23, 36, 38
Funeral practices, 14, 22, *22*, 32, 38, *39*, 40–41, *40–41*

Geological epochs and glaciations, chart of, *11*, 11
Gibraltar, 9

Homo erectus, 9, 17

Homo sapiens sapiens, 17
Aurignacian culture, 16
skull of, 9, *9*
Horsetail (*Equistum arvense*), 20, *20*
Hunting, 13, 22, 25, 36

Kebara, Israel, 41
Kheit Qasim, Iraq, 22
Krapina, Croatia, 16, 22

La Chapelle-aux-Saints, Corrèze, France, 9, 13
La Ferrassie, Dordogne, France, 23, 35, 40
Le Moustier, Dordogne, France, 33
Le Régourdou, France, 41
Levallois technique, 14, 30, 31

Mammoths, 36, *36–37*
Marmots, *24*, 24, 25
Mezhirich, Ukraine, 37
Mezin, Ukraine, 39
Mimbres Indians, 22
Minerals, 26, 27, *27*
Moldova, Ukraine, 37
Monte Circeo, Italy, 28, 40
Morvan, France, 27
Mousterian culture, 14
Musical instruments, 14, 15, *15*

Neanderthal man
coexistence with *Homo sapiens sapiens*, 16
dwellings of, 13, 32, *32–33*
evolution of, 9
extinction of, 17
fire, use of, 14, 26
food, 23, 36, 38
funeral practices of, 9, 14, 22, *22*, 32, 38, *39*, 40–41, *40–41*
hunting and, 13, 22, 25, 36
mandible of, 23, *23*
migration of, 13
Mousterian culture, 14

name, 8
skull of, 8, 9, *9*, 10, *12*, 13, *16*, 16, *22*, 22, *40*, 40
tools and weapons of, 14, *14*, 28, 28–31, *29*, *30*, 35, *35*
Neanderthal Valley, Düsseldorf, Germany, 9

Ochre powder, 14, 38, 39

Pavlov Mountains, Czech Republic, 37
Peking observatory, *43*, 43
Pleistocene period, 24
Pre-Neanderthal man, 9
Pyrite, 26, 27, *27*

Quartz, 26, 27, *27*

Rainbow Cave, Arcy-sur-Cure, France, 35
Rock painting, *24*, 24, 39

Saccopastore, Italy, 16, 28
Saint-Césaire, France, 16
Serpentine, 26, 27, *27*
Shanidar, Iraq, 14, 20
Skull of Galilee, 17, *17*
Skull of Neanderthal man, 8, 9, *9*, 10, *12*, 13, *16*, 16, *22*, 22, *40*, 40
Snakes, 20, *20*
Stars, 42, *42*, 43
Stonehenge, England, *42*, 43
Stoneknapping, 14

Teshik-Tash, Uzbekistan, 41
Tools and weapons, 14, *14*, 28, 28–31, *29*, *30*, 35, *35*

Ursus spelaeus (cave bear), skull of, *32*, 33

Val Camonica, Italy, 24

Würm Ice Age, 9

Yarrow, 16, *16*

ILLUSTRATION SOURCES

*The number in boldface refers to the page, and the number
in parentheses refers to the illustration.*

CRISTIANO DAL SASSO: **20** (1), **24**, (1), **36** (1). EDITORIALE JACA BOOK (Astrofili Italiani): **42** (1); (Giorgio Bacchin)
23 (5); (Alessandro Baldanzi): **10** (1), **11** (2, 3); (Alessandro Bartolozzi): **8** (2); (Remo Berselli): **17** (5); (Dulio Citi): **28**
(1); (Sandro Corsi): **42** (2); (Il Fotogramma): **30** (1, 2, 3, 4); (Jorio): **17** (4); (Antonio Molino) **41** (4); (Lorenzo Orlandi):
20 (2, 3); (Michela Rangoni Machiavelli): **14** (4, 5, 6), **15**; (Carlo Scotti): **26**, (1, 2), **27** (3), **32** (2); (Angelo Stabin): **27**
(4), **43** (4). PEDRO A. SAURA RAMOS: **39** (3). ARIBERTO SEGALA: **24** (5).

Illustration sources faithfully reproduced or modified

Anati, Emmanuel. *The Imaginary Museum of Prehistory. Rock Art of the World.* Jaca Book, 2002: **24** (3)

Anati, Emmanuel. *Origins of Art and Conceptuality.* Jaca Book, 1989: **40** (1).

Beltrán, Antonio. *From Hunters to Breeders: Cave Art of the East of Spain.* Jaca Book, 1979: **24** (2).

Bonnier, Gaston, and Robert Douin. *The Complete Illustrated Flora of France, Switzerland and Belgium in Color.* Illustrated by Julie Poinsot, Editions Belin, 1990 [Italian translation Jaca Book, 1995]: **33** (4).

Broglio, Alberto and Janusz Kozlowski. *Paleolithic Age.* Jaca Book, 1986: **34** (1), **35** (2).

Dué, Andrea, edited by. *The First Inhabited Lands. From Primates to Homo Sapiens.* Vol.1 of *The Atlases of the History of Mankind.* Jaca Book, 1993: **30** (6), **31**(7).

Dué, Andrea, edited by. *In Prehistoric Times*, Vol. 1 of *The Historical Atlases. Man and the Environment.* Jaca Book, 1997: **10-11** (5).

Facchini, Fiorenzo. *The Path of Human Evolution.* Jaca Book, 1994: **8** (1), **9** (5), **22** (1).

Facchini, Fiorenzo. *Origins: Man. Introduction to Paleoanthropology.* Jaca Book, 1990: **12-13, 16** (2, 3), **28** (2), **32** (1).

Facchini, Fiorenzo, edited by. *Paleoanthropology and Prehistory,* a volume of *The Open Thematic Encyclopedia.* Jaca Book, 1993: **28** (3), **29** (4), **37** (4).

Forest, Jean-Daniel. *Mesopotamia: The Invention of the State.* Jaca Book, 1996: **22** (3).

Giacobini, Giacomo, and Francesco D'Errico. "The Last Neanderthals and the First Modern Humans in Europe," in *The Human Adventure.* Jaca Book, Year 1, no. 3, winter, 1986–1987: **29** (5).

Giacobini, Giacomo, edited by. *The Neanderthal Hunters.* Jaca Book, 1986: **14** (1), **21** (5), **23** (6), **30** (5), **35** (3, 4), **36** (2), **41** (3, 5).

González Licón, Ernesto. *Three Thousand Years of Precolumbian Civilization. The Zapotecs and Mixtecs.* Jaca Book, 1991: **24** (4).

Kozlowski, Janusz K. *Prehistory of Eastern European Art.* Jaca Book, 1992: **22** (2), **39** (4).

Kozlowski, Janusz K. "The Mammoth Hunters," in *The Human Adventure.* Jaca Book, Year 5, no. 17, summer, 1991: **36** (3).

Leroi-Gourhan, André. *Europe's Oldest Artists: An Introduction to Paleolithic Cave Wall Art.* Jaca Book, 1981: **39** (2).

Pinna, Giovanni, edited by. *Natural History of Europe. Six Hundred Million Years Through the Great Paleontological Sites.* Jaca Book, 1999: **27** (6).

Renault-Miskowsky, Josette. *The Environment During Prehistoric Times.* Masson Editeur, Paris, 1986. [Italian translation by Jaca Book, 1987]: **10** (1), **11** (2, 3, 4), **27** (5).

*Other pictures not mentioned here come from the Jaca Book archives.
Alessandro Baldanzi is the author of those tables not mentioned here.*